Help Me Adapt, Lord

Judith Mattison

Discovering New Blessings While Learning to Live with Less

AUGSBURG Publishing House • Minneapolis

HELP ME ADAPT, LORD

Library of Congress Catalog Card No. 80-67797

International Standard Book No. 0-8066-1859-0

Photos: David Strickler, 10, 41; Rohn Engh, 23; Bob Combs, 32; Camerique, 51, 66, 92; David Hiebert, 55; Jean-Claude Lejeune, 59; Louis C. Williams, 72; Freda Leinwand, 79; Paul Wychor, 85.

Manufactured in the United States of America

This book has been guided
by the faith, creativity, and vision
of my friend
Roland Seboldt.
Thanks to him.

Contents

How much is enough?

My life has gone along well
    regular raises
    home improvements
    happy vacations.
Enough,
always enough.
Just lately I've cause to wonder.
Will it all be different soon?
Will I always have a car
    new clothes
    cheap housing
    a raise?
Will I have to adapt to change,
adjust my expectations,
temper my extravagances,
be satisfied with less?
Will "less" be enough?

Lord, you have spoken to me
of an abundant life.
Not so much the surplus
of affluence,
but the joys of love—
serving, caring,
learning about life and you.
This new life
does not rely on things
but finds satisfaction in being
    doing justice
    valuing people.
The abundant life knows contentment
and there is always enough.

When I need a lift

When I feel "down" or bored
I often go shopping—
    look around
    see what's new
    pick up a little something.
It gives me a lift
at least temporarily.
I've done it for years.

Lately I've found I spend less money
if I don't use stores
as my "happiness tonic."
Being in stores
tends to whet my appetite
for more possessions.
Everything begins to look necessary
    clever
    cute
    attractive
    needed.
Happiness comes from within me,
not from what I see or own.
I can get a richer lift
from a walk or a book
or by calling a friend.
It's more wholesome,
economical, and real.

New is a magic word

New.
It's a magic word
used to boost sales of
soap and cars
and headache formulas,
and it appeals to my desire
to experience excitement
and avoid routine or satisfaction.
I'm encouraged to decry boredom
and demand constant change.
New!

Everything cannot be new.
Nor can life be
one adventure after another,
flashy and exciting.
There are good qualities to the
familiar and old,
repetition and routine
which I can treasure too.
In last year's styles
and our aging car,
among familiar friendships
and the security of routine,
I can find contentment
because every breath of life
is another adventure.
In God, each day is new.

Garage sales

Garage sales
used to be
a diversion.
Fun to buy and sell—
make a little extra money.
Casting off the old—
sold!
Disposing of the hardly used
to make room for the new.
Buy—sell—buy.
More and more.

Now a garage sale
is less frivolity,
more necessity—
a handy, economical way
to recycle and share.
Buy—sell—repair.
Use again.
We will have fun and
save a little extra money.
We do not hastily cast away,
but value the opportunity
to keep and share,
and use more fully what is ours.

A fine suit

You can spot
a finely tailored suit.
It fits well—
    matched plaids
    even shoulders
    careful weave.
It wears well
and feels good.

A finely tailored person
looks good in any suit,
    standing tall in self-respect
    unpretentious
    making careful choices
    fair.
Woven of godly nature,
such a person wears well,
lasting.

Sports car

Ever since the '50s
he's dreamed of owning a sports car.
The dream was delayed,
and now denied.
Priorities and the cost of cars
prohibit the realization of his dream.

He has adapted.
He loves to tinker with cars,
so he bought an old car—
a semisport model
in need of much care.
He will be busy for months (years!)
    reconditioning
    painting
    planning
    dreaming.
He has adjusted his dream
to an attainable,
more humble goal.
The joy is in the act
of reaching for
and achieving a goal,
not in the product itself.
Doing replaces having.

Out of gas

A long drive.
A near-empty gas tank.
There's a station!
We pull in to find the sign
Out of Gas.
Mixed emotions—
        disappointment
        frustration
        anger!
I'm angry because I can't have my way—
now!
I'm angry because some people waste gas
or "top off" their tanks
to be on the safe side,
and now I have none.
I'm angry that we ignored predictions
and now we live with
too little, too late.
My anger passes
as I try to find
enough gas to get home.
I admit I'm part of the problem too.
We all continue to overconsume
and sometimes blame others
rather than change ourselves.
Blaming others is a waste of energy.
Help us change
before we're completely
out of gas.

We have a car pool

It seemed like a hassle—
car pool!
Sublimating independence,
planning ahead,
locating riders.
But necessity dictated,
and we learned a new way.
Morning is now friendly
and afternoon relaxing
as we ride together
    talk and joke
    share driving
    hassle less traffic.
We've exchanged independence
for friendship
and we've come out ahead.

Summer travel is fun

One of our best family times
is a summer vacation trip.
Relaxed.
Together.
Long drives through our
spacious land.
This year we can't afford to go.
Disappointment.
Frustration.
Anger at the increased costs
of fuel and accommodations.

Is it any less a vacation
if we travel closer to home?
Is beauty only in distant places?
Or are we capable of discovering
excitement and pleasure
in more commonplace experiences—
  an emerging butterfly
  a sunrise
  the children's jokes.
Relaxed.
Together.

Mom and Pop stores

I hear that someone in our area
is opening a small grocery store.
I'm delighted!
I'm tired of asphalt parking lots
and driving to a distant mall.
I rather enjoy a walk
to a nearby store—
running into neighbors,
finding fresh fruit
without plastic wrap.
I can still benefit
from the convenience of
large store shopping
from time to time.
But I need not run to the distant store,
hassle the crowds,
use valuable gas
for a small purchase.
It's like stepping back into the '20s or '30s.
Perhaps a step backward
can be a step forward!

I'm learning patience

I'm not always patient.
I like to arrive on time
or get things done
to satisfy my immediate wants.
Riding a bus is slower,
and finding a friend takes time.
I'm impatient.

I have to slow down now.
I ride buses rather than drive.
It takes more time.
But it means I can read a good book
or observe other people
(they are so interesting!).
I can sort out my thoughts
and meet fellow riders.
I'm saving fuel
and finding friends
and learning to be
patient.

Roadways

Airplane view.
Concrete roadway designs.
Long curving lines,
intricate patterns of
        overpass
        cloverleaf.
For decades
we have carved our inscriptions of concrete
across green and fertile land.
This was our legacy,
our tribute to cheap petroleum.
We gobbled gas as if there were no limits.
But limits have risen on our horizon
and concrete looks less inviting,
more severe.
Now we will choose to build better roadways
toward a well-fed world
and interdependence,
toward preserving life-giving soil,
recognizing that limits do indeed exist
and that God will be with us
as we construct new roads.

Water is precious

The water runs
    as I wash and rinse dishes
    as I am distracted
    as I linger a while in the shower.
The water runs,
the heat dissipates,
the liquid disappears.

I saw the library poster:
"All the water on earth
is all the water there is."
Some people have water
    contaminated
    restricted.
I have water
    heated
    handy
    fresh and pure.
"All the water on earth
is all the water there is."
Turn my mind on
and the water off
unless I really need it.

The earth loves me

The earth is meant
to be my home—
comfort
protection.
God's world loves me,
rocks me in natural rhythms,
caresses me with breezes,
feeds me with air and plants,
soothes me with snow,
and warms me with sun.
I have forgotten,
distracted by alien structures
and forbidding concrete.
I need the earth.
I need its love
more than I need man-made stone.

Lord, I'm anxious

Sometimes I worry.
What about our retirement
    our children's futures
    the world's shifting economy?
I'm anxious.
I'm anxious because
I don't know
how it will all work out.

You speak across the centuries,
telling me that anxiety
is inevitable,
part of life—
and in our day,
anxiety is to be expected.
But as you assured the Israelites,
you assure me, God,
that you are the power.
Jesus understood.
He wasn't always sure
how it would work out,
but he trusted
that whatever happened
you'd be there.

Is it gain or loss?

It feels like giving up—
no more long drives
    extra movies
    polyester convenience
    luxury
    glamour
    TV dinners.

Yet another tally shows
it is a gain—
    time to talk things over
    fewer hungry people
    grass
    quiet
    cooperation with friends.

I lose the excess
but I gain the real.

I need self-discipline

I respect disciplined people
 scholars
 runners
 gymnasts
 monks.
They concentrate;
they focus on their important issue
and maintain a consistent
habit or pursuit.
Their pride is in doing it well.

Can I be more self-disciplined?
I want to focus
on the issues of my day—
 conservation
 shared resources
 long-range choices.
The way to do it is to develop
 habits
 thought processes
 alternative values
and concentrate on keeping them.
The reward will be self-respect
and the pride of doing good.

What is really necessary?

Make a list of needs:
    new coat
    family room
    microwave
    swimming suit
    higher salary
    color TV.
Stop.
Think it over.
Make a list of needs:
    warm coat
    good roof
    decent food
    clean water
    a job
    rest
    quiet
    someone who cares.
Wisdom of the fathers:
"He has showed you, O man, what is good."

Eating out

We used to eat out a lot.
We appreciated the variety,
the relief from cooking and sameness.
We have to change now.
We can't afford supper out
as often as before.
When we have a chance to get away
we choose a low-cost meal.

I can accept this change
because it has advantages.
Going out to eat is a special event
rather than familiar and expected.
I feel better when I eat moderately
(I was uncomfortable when I couldn't finish
all the food served
at an elaborate steak restaurant).
I'm more creative in my cooking,
a satisfying accomplishment.
Change helps me develop my skills
and appreciate life.

Convenience foods

Frankly, I love convenience foods
for the time they save
for their ease of preparation
for the availability of off-season food.
It's a wonder of our age!
I hate to give them up.

The sooner I adjust that attitude
the better off everyone will be.
It's a huge energy cost
to transport fresh food cross-country
to fast-freeze products
to package elaborately.
Think it over.
Grandma and Mother got along,
I can do it too.
I kind of enjoy baking bread—
the accomplishment, the pride—
from scratch!
I can use my intelligence
to learn about nutrition
and know that my family will be
healthier, stronger,
perhaps even more intelligent.
Attitudes and buying habits
can be adjusted.
I pray for strength and wisdom
to do just that.
Help me, Lord.
I need you.

Company's coming!

I always fuss
when company comes—
    cleaning
    fresh flowers
    careful plans for a special meal.
People appreciate the effort.
The table
and our bodies
groan under the weight of food—
    meat
    rich sauces
    fancy dessert.
Then we sit at the table and talk,
sometimes for hours.
We share ourselves around the board.

Recently we've discovered
it's just as much fun
to have a simpler meal—
soup, salad, sandwiches.
I'm less harried, more relaxed.
Our bodies don't feel stuffed.
We still have the best part—
long talks around the table.
Simpler and satisfying.

Teach children values

I want to teach my children
lasting values—
    Christian
    caring
    unselfish
    kind.
I'm impatient when they
beg for more things
or leave lights burning.
How do I persuade children—
present-day people—
that tomorrow will reflect today?
That blessed people are to be good stewards?
That people are more important than things?

I teach them by example:
    buying less or delaying purchases
    repairing, recycling
    contrasting profit with people motives
    spending time with them playing games
    rejoicing in what we have
    rather than complaining about our lack.
I must expect no more of them
than I expect of myself.

What can I do about world hunger?

Hunger.
What do I know of hunger?
Temporary pangs between meals.
Hunger saps strength,
    energy
    brainpower
    the will to live.
Lord, it is a sin
that your creatures,
any of them,
should lack the will to *live*—
your great gift!—
because they're hungry,
while others are overfed.
Even though grocery prices are higher,
I am fed.

There are things I can do
and learn
to help change this world,
to feed the many,
to share.
But it's a complicated job,
so I delay or deny or idly hope.
The job,
the people
wait . . .
for me.
Lord, we do not lack the strength.
We lack the *will.*

I like being independent

I've grown self-sufficient.
I flaunt independence
in the face of God's plan
in the guise of
bootstrap success,
impenetrable self-control,
and the claim to
my rights—
to drive when and where I please,
to spend money as I choose,
to look out for number one,
to be the best
    at work
    at play
    perhaps even in my church.
Nobody tells me what to do!
Superior.
Stubborn.
Self-serving.
The price I shall pay
is isolation.
Independently alone.

Poverty is relative

When I feel poor
I open a book
and look at pictures
of the rest of the world—
the children of Calcutta,
the women of Ethiopia,
the men of Mexico.
Poverty is relative,
and I am not one of the world's poor.
If I spend my time
thinking about the upper crust
and envying them,
I forget that a crust of bread
would sustain a person
a few hours longer
if I would share it.
As near as Detroit
and Appalachia
is the rope of poverty
which strangles hope and
determination.
Look again at the pictures.
I am not poor.

When guilt weighs me down

I'm tripping over guilt these days.
I know the truth of
    overindulgence
    underdevelopment
    hunger
    exploitation of the powerless
and the temptation
to want to forget all that
and keep everything for ourselves.
Guilt catches my step
and I sprawl awkwardly
in the mud of selfishness.

Stand up.
Clean up!
God puts me back on my feet—
forgiven.
I'm not perfect.
(Had I thought I was?)
I'm washed clean
and left with a job to do—
    to notice
    to share
    to conserve
    to preserve
    to care
while walking humbly with my God.

Sacrifice is hard

I really don't know much
of sacrifice.
We hear the word a lot,
especially during Lent,
but we've seldom had to
get beyond the word
to the experience.
I am beginning to see
I'll have to sacrifice more,
if not for my children,
then for my nation.
God has told me about sacrifice
throughout the Scriptures.
From Abraham and Isaac
to Jesus and Stephen and Paul,
we learn that God expects
sacrifice.
Like athletes who train,
we develop ourselves—
    our will to do good
    our trust of God's purposes
    our ability to give.
Sacrifice changes me
from a rebellious, self-serving creature
to a faithful, dedicated servant.
Sacrifice brings me
closer to God.

Am I all alone?

Sometimes I feel like I'm the only one
who drives within the speed limit
who conserves heat in winter
who tries to live with less.
It's no fun.
I can't even get much satisfaction
from feeling self-righteous,
especially when friends
wear the latest fashions
or buy a new gadget appliance.
I feel alone.

I need support—
friends like me who try,
who have ideas for practical conservation.
I could find them, I'm sure,
if I asked around a bit,
shared my ideas.
I know you support me, Lord.
Lead me to people who care.

Neighborhood work crew

We've started a neighborhood work crew.
Everyone has different skills
    or tools
    or time
and together we work on projects
which can't be done alone—
    a paint job
    heavy cleaning
    some roofing
    a minor plumbing change.
We did it to save money,
but we've discovered more—
    deeper friendships
    stronger trust
    interdependence.
It feels good
to need each other,
to have something to give.
We've discovered
neighbors.

Should I lead the way?

Cooperation.
It sounds easier
than it happens.
It takes one person,
a risk-taker,
to offer to
    share
    lead
    suggest a way.
Others join in
and cooperation begins.
Once begun, the benefits are clear—
    camaraderie
    shared work
    mutual decisions
    larger goals.
Someone has to be the first to offer.
Is it me, Lord?

It's showtime!

Everybody got together
in the yard of a mutual friend.
An evening out.
We watched a terrific show!—

a duet by twins
a guitar solo by Jim
Marge's kitchen band
a crazy men's quartet
Bobby's original poem
an acrobatic demonstration
by all the elementary kids

and a finale of saints marchin' in.
Then, inspired by crickets,
we sang old songs
and hymns
till late.
A wonderful show of the
wealth of human creative talents,
sailing free in the August night.

I wish we could move

Oh, I wish we could move!
Our house seems crowded.
When we bought it,
I remember thinking
it was an adequate house,
one to last a lifetime.
It is.
A nice, pleasant home.
But I guess deep-down I thought
if we wanted to
we could move someday.
We can't.

Look around me.
Make a list:
    warm rooms and floors
    ample furniture
    a nice yard
    close to transportation
    walk to church, to stores.
A nice, pleasant home.
Add a touch of color
    some plants
    some fresh paint
    rearranging
    reupholstering
    gratitude.
Deep down I am glad to have
a nice, pleasant home.

Furnishing a home

I've been in some lovely homes.
Each is different—
    orderly colonial
    spacious and contemporary
    quaint, cottagelike
    stately, with polished dark woodwork.
It's a pleasant experience.
Many homes are perfectly furnished,
with matching period pieces
    fine china
    elegant carpeting.
When I leave homes like that
I'm dissatisfied,
disappointed in my home.
I wish I could have
what others have.

If I'm honest I know
that keeping up with the Joneses
isn't "other people's" problem—
it's mine.
It's self-defeating
and doesn't keep my heart
on important matters.
People are more important than things.

An extra bedroom

We thought we'd add an extra bedroom
as soon as the children grew bigger.
We knew we'd be
colliding in the bathroom
and competing for space someday.
The reality is
we won't ever have that room.
We can't afford to build or heat it.

Then we remembered that when we were young
our homes were small,
and no one expected more.
We scheduled the bathroom
and shared the space.
We made room for friends
and enjoyed feeling cozy
rather than running away
to private grottos.

When the children are gone
we won't "need" the space.
And we won't have to heat an extra room.
We'll heat our small house
with love.

Our world is crowded

The buildings of our future
will be increasingly vertical.
We'll have to share
walls and heat
so we'll gather in
our horizontal sprawl
and stack ourselves taller.
I don't like the idea.
It's confining.

Yet life is not a sprawl.
It needs intention, focus, meaning.
We may lose open space
but gain the ability
to get along better
    accept differences
    discover cooperative skills.
Life is constructed
of relationships.
Our towers need not be like Babel.
We can cooperate
and enjoy each other,
growing spiritually tall
as we construct lives
of human caring.

We fear the unknown

He felt depressed.
A heart attack left him
afraid
unsure.
"It's the unknown," he said.
We understood.

We have constant changes
less water
fewer cars
costly mortgages.
Our economy
and way of life
changes and rearranges
and we feel insecure.
We fear losing the familiar
and are afraid of the unknown.

Long ago you knew, Lord,
that people fear unknowns
and seek security.
Then you said,
"Trust in me."
Now we hear you again.
We understand.

Basking in summer sun

The sun is out—
Glory!
Warm, cheerful, welcome.
We look for shade
beneath a comforting tree
and relax, peaceful.
Birds converse
and the grass is cool.
What machine
or humanly contrived entertainment
can match the simple goodness
of sun and shade.
Glory.

Sports can be fun

Sports—our great pastime.
We enthusiastically support
the efforts of teams and individuals.
In our country
more than any other
we love athletics.
Over the years we have devoted
great sums of money
to the pursuit of sports.
Hundreds of dollars are spent on
    hockey skates
    baseball uniforms
    basketball tickets
    Super Bowl ads.
We have organized children's games
and established complex park and
school programs.
Perhaps changing our life-styles will
reduce our ability to buy
elaborate equipment
and costly tickets.
We will rediscover the pleasure
of a pick-up game of softball,
a neighborhood volleyball tourney,
and a hilarious afternoon of
shooting basketballs into a hoop,
with no equipment but a ball,
and virtually no expense.
Playing rather than watching,
cooperative joy
rather than competition.
Fun and games.

Are we slaves of pleasure?

Without realizing
we've become slaves of pleasure.
We expect it—
    good weather
    no boredom
    big production numbers
    300 horsepower motors.
When we're bored or broke
we lament our lot,
frantic for fun
or activity.
We substitute speed
for personal achievement
and passive viewing
for good, clean fun.

We can change—
free ourselves
from this false expectation,
find spontaneity again.
People don't need frantic fun.
They need friends
and challenges
and God.

It's time to pay bills

I pile them up on the desk,
one bill after another.
Payments due.
I'm discouraged.
There isn't enough this month.
I feel angry.
Why is there never enough?

Perhaps there is never enough
because people are never satisfied.
We always think we want more,
we're missing something,
"if only . . . ."
When there was more money
we sought more things
and made a lot of
foolish purchases.
Now there is less money,
and I continue to think
it's someone else's fault
or that more money would solve
the problem.
The problem is me.
I don't always think through
my spending choices,
nor do I like to wait for desires.

Make a pile of papers
with blessings listed on each.
The desktop overflows.
Pay the bills and start again.
I have enough.

Change is exhilarating!

Every now and then
I feel exhilarated by change.
I've experienced such genuine satisfactions
in recent months.
I feel less driven,
more healthy.
I'm working to improve myself—
    walking more
    eating better foods.
I have more time for friends
and time to listen to children.
Clocks don't intimidate me as they used to.
I've grown more skillful in prioritizing
    time
    interests
    personal values.
I think the exhilaration comes from
more than personal pride.
I think it is a sense of being
in closer harmony with your plan.
Joy.

Volunteers are important

We used to admire volunteers.
Theirs was noble service.
Somehow we lost our vision,
and nobility was replaced
with mobility
and a nagging need to be paid
in order to feel worthwhile.
If I'm not salaried
am I any less capable
or able to contribute?
Is it a paycheck
that gives me satisfaction,
or is it a job well done?
I am created to give
even without return.
My reward
is my personal sense of pride
in doing something well
for someone else.
If someone needs my help
I'll volunteer.

We all risk unemployment

Unemployment
lurks in our neighborhood.
It's an unspoken fear
as we see our economy shift
and adapt to change.
Each woman or man hopes
    "not me"
    "not my industry"
    "I need to have a job."
Perhaps the hardest part
is that we don't talk about it
and we feel powerless.

But you've given us better options, Lord.
We can anticipate change
so that if it comes
we can take charge
    make decisions
    find other work
    adjust our spending.
We can encourage business and government
to help us redistribute work loads
    hours
    skills.
And we can share our fears,
talk to each other,
help each other
find creative solutions,
stand by our friends and neighbors.
If we work at it
we can manage even unemployment
with your support.

It's a disposable society

It's been a throwaway world.
Disposable
    diapers
    tableware
    cups
    shavers
    dressing gowns
    pop cans
    bedpans
    tissues.
Castoffs creating landfills,
landfills of luxury.

Soon it became pervasive.
Cast-off people.
Disposable values.
Replaceable nature.

Shall we yet throw away
all that is dear?
Or will we cling to
lasting, life-giving values?
    People
    love
    sharing
    earth
    God.

We all need limits

I've always resisted limits.
Diets, discipline—
they're hard to maintain.
It's the same old story—
people rebel against God
    rationalize
    resist
    take the forbidden fruit.
Yet I know I need limits.
Everybody does.
We aren't comfortable when we
    overindulge
    act wastefully
    rationalize
    overlook injustice.
Perhaps we are afraid of ourselves
and what untempered desire
can do to the world
and to us.
As our lives simplify
and we peel away excess,
we may discover God's fruits of life—
    firm
    sweet
    limited
but good.

A ball of string

A big ball of string
kept in a corner—
Grandpa's statement about waste.
Hazel saved soap chips
to send abroad,
and Mom flattened wartime tin cans.
Most of our children have only known
    paper plates
    plastic forks
    disposable diapers
    aluminum cans.
Times are changing.
A church circle collects aluminum,
the neighbors have kept their old chair.
Shelley won't buy plastic cups anymore.
I'm learning to fix my own lamp.
Grandpa used to say:
Waste not,
want not.
He knew what he was talking about.

Do I need new shoes?

My comfortable shoes
are wearing thin.
The soles are worn
and the scuffs show.
Time for another pair.
Or is it?
Perhaps I could
recycle rather than replace.
New soles and polish
would suffice.
Part of understanding life
is recognizing limits
and expanding creativity.
I can resole
and resoul.

I've got a new bike

I waited for my first bike
Until I was fourteen.
It was forever—
or so it seemed.
Shiny and new,
I would have been satisfied
with old and dented.
I loved that bike.
I was free to go, at last!

Here I am,
ready to buy my second bike.
Older,
I'm no less excited.
I intend to use it often
for shopping trips
        exercise
        family outings.
It can be old or dented,
it won't matter.
I might never have had this
second bicycle
if there'd been no energy crisis
or changing life-styles.
Lucky me!
Again, I'm free!

Creative fun

On a brisk winter day
the teenagers on a retreat
ran outdoors to play.
No equipment
    except for hills
    and snow
    and people.
So they joined hands
and ran in wavy lines
    up and down
    laughing
    falling—
"Crack the Whip" in the snow.
Joyous recreation!
With only their ingenuity to rely on
they entertained themselves
in a chain of creative friendship
and fun!

Christmas outlook

Department stores are gearing up—
    subtle signs
    October hints
    harbingers of holidays.
They want me to start to plan,
to expand my "want" list
and my gift list.
Purchaseable tokens of love.

I can change.
I can focus on the meaning of a
Christian Christmas,
cut my gift list,
increase my phone call
and visiting list.
Friends can't be purchased
and visits are more memorable
than trinkets or toys.
I don't need
all the things I'm tempted to want.
I can make gifts,
and as I do,
concentrate on the cause of Christmas—
that God gave me
the privilege of loving
and living
in his Son.
Not purchaseable,
but genuine and lasting.

Children's Christmas

This year we made all our gifts.
Tree ornaments for friends and neighbors,
candy for Grandma, scarves for Jean,
food for the birds,
candles for Sis, and
a stone paperweight for Uncle Jim.
It took more time—
or did it?
The best part was opening day.
The giver was as thrilled as the receiver!
We laughed
    chattered
    tried on
    exclaimed!
Afterward we all played table games—
every age, all abilities
together.
The children came to me, smiling.
"Let's do that again next year."
And we will!

Help me take time

Sometimes the lord of my life
is the clock.
Check my watch,
survey the wall.
Time to go.
Time to run.
Move on, keep traveling,
next appointment, hurry, late.
I am bound in thoughts of time.
I choose my activities
    my friends
    my vehicle
    my priorities
based on how much time it takes.

Friendships are enriched
only if we take time to nurture them.
Staying longer, listening—
these are the time-consuming choices
but the decisions which offer
meaning to life.

Slow down.
Walk to the store.
Listen to the children.
Take time to stay for coffee.
Eliminate some activities.
Time is but a tally of moments.
Life is what we give
to the precious time we have.

Walking the dog

I walked the dog.
The air was fresh, crisp;
the night, quiet.
My muscles stretched, relaxed.
Through a window I saw
    father and son
    bent forward
    intent on chess
    content.
I heard the rustle
    of leaves
    and nature.
Cars did not intrude,
nor radios,
and the world gave me
peace.
An unhurried moment,
savored.
This life,
neither hasty
nor plastic,
is good.

Family entertainment

We used to roll out down the driveway
headed for a change of scene.
An afternoon drive.
Everyone was there
    laughing
    looking
    talking
    bantering back and forth.
We'd sometimes sing,
stop for a meal,
turn around and drive home.
Family entertainment.

Now we roll out the green
of our Ping-Pong table.
Everyone is there
    laughing
    playing
    talking
bantering and bouncing back and forth.
Sometimes we have a contest
or stop for a meal.
And all the while
we are at home!
Family entertainment.

Making time for Grandma

Driving hurriedly through town,
on my way to another commitment
or social event,
aloud I say,
"It's a crazy world
when I don't have time
to visit Grandma."
I'm too busy.

What's wrong with a world
when there's no time left
for love?
I look forward to change.
I shall pare down my life—
    fewer meetings
    less running
    less paper and chatter
    less food.
I shall begin now
before Grandma and her love
are gone.

What does Easter mean?

When I was young
a new Easter bonnet
was a happy part of spring.
We don't wear hats much anymore,
but a new dress or shoes
have still been part of the celebration.

I can't afford a new dress
or hat or shoes,
and probably I don't need them.
I can celebrate Easter
in a different way—
a new scarf,
a fresh carnation,
or better,
a new outlook
from where I am,
satisfied with what I have,
glad to be alive,
grateful that Jesus lives
always, again and again.
Happy rebirth in spring.

I'm frustrated!

Frustration
is such an upsetting feeling!
These days I get large doses of it
as goods are less available,
travel times are longer,
and I can't find
a small appliance repair shop.
Frustration!
I'm accustomed to speed and ease.

I can't eliminate this gradual shift
from uninhibited fulfillment
of my desires and goals.
I have to adjust rather than
waste precious personal strength
on clenched fists
and churning brains
or stomach.
I will not succumb to frustration.

God gave me life and
life is too good to waste
on resisting reality
in the name of having all my desires
    in my own way
    my own time.
I choose to adjust.

Small closets

The charm of an old house
has often been diminished by
the disappointment of small closets.
Storage space—
we need more room for things.

Now my world changes
and I have fewer things.
As it was in Grandma's house,
smaller closets are sufficient.
I don't need a different dress
for every different event or day.
I may even return again to
one Sunday-best dress.
It will be enough
because I will be covered
    warm
    well groomed
and because my clothes
do not make me more worthy
    more important
    "better"
    secure
    whole.
You, Lord, do all that.

I learned to upholster

A threadbare chair.
Time for a change.
I took a class,
learned to upholster,
and did it myself!
It was a life-giving experience
    discovery of ability
    training a skill
    valuing the old
    creating something new.
A few mistakes
but, in general,
success and growth.
Reupholding
the gift of meaningful life.

Do-it-yourself skills

Ouch!
I missed the nail again.
More often I hit it
at a slant
and have to take it out
and start over.
Mistakes.
Repetition.
Do it yourself is cheaper,
but it's also very frustrating!

Slow down.
Be patient with myself.
Skills are to be learned
    acquired
    practiced.
They aren't always easy
or natural.
On the other hand,
I've learned new things before
and I'm able to do so again.
I'll feel good about myself
if I have the perseverance
to keep trying.
It's like a first grader
learning how to read.
An adventure.
Not always perfect,
but learning from my mistakes.
A lesson for living.

Recycling project

There's a debate at church.
A group wants to collect
aluminum and glass.
They want to recycle
as an example to others
that our church commends
a conservative, humble life-style.
Some members aren't sure.
It's not neat.
It's a big job
needing lots of volunteers.
Does this project belong in the church?

Help us, Lord, to see our church
less as a museum,
more as a working clinic
    healing the sick
    helping the weak
    teaching the world.
A living message to the world
that we care about people,
the earth,
and God's plan.

Help us take care

Our history with land
is one of possessing.
We went west
    conquered
    settled
    carved into sections.
Now we claim plots
and lots,
build a fence,
and label land "mine."

Who owns the oceans? the sky?
Who owned the trees, the mountains
before the "settlers" came?
The Sioux knew
land is God's
and mountains belong to all.
What we have,
we have temporarily,
and we are intended to share.
We are caretakers,
not owners.
God is the gracious giver.
We receive and share
in thanks,
and it is up to us
to take care.

Give us vision, Lord

A letter from Sweden
spoke of confusion—
experts disagreeing.
The choices:
unemployment or
25 years of nuclear power—
then a moratorium.
We, too, shall face their choices:
How shall we decide?

Give us long-range vision, Lord:
from pyramids to the future—
5000 years back and forward
and our small moment of time
in the middle of it.
What will our choices mean
to people of the future?
Will we leave a legacy
of wonder, like pyramids—
monuments that amaze?
Or will we leave
monuments of fear?
Help us realize that our choices
are not for us alone,
but for all humans
and for years to come.

We're number one

I'm used to it—
being number one.
I don't win everything,
but I'm used to being on top.
Line up the evidence:
    powerful country
    middle class
    literate.
Power.
First.

The problem is
we sometimes view first
as right
and power as deserved
or superiority
rather than as a call
to greater responsibility.
"Every one to whom much is given,
of him will much be required."

Lord, number one means
"share with others."
The first must be last
and responsible.
You're number one.
We need humility.

Who can I trust?

Lately I'm more suspicious.
I wonder if other people
get more than their share
or take advantage.
Is someone else making money
as I sacrifice and conserve?
Can I trust other people
    to share
    or care—about me?

Mistrust is a human frailty
rooted in self-preservation
and self-centeredness.
It makes people paranoid
and paranoia is contagious.
Stand back
and laugh at ourselves.
This is a time when we need
cooperation instead of paranoia,
giving rather than suspicion.
Trust builds trust.
If I want sharing
I must offer it.

Welcoming refugees

For decades immigrants came
to our welcoming shores.
They worked
    learned
    developed this land.
Refugees
bringing desire and strength.
We are diverse and strong
because they came.

Now that we have so much,
let us look back
in gratitude
and welcome more immigrants.
New people
offering greater diversity
and additional strengths.
We do not choose
to keep only for ourselves.
We choose to share
because we have much
and it is right
to give refugees
a home.

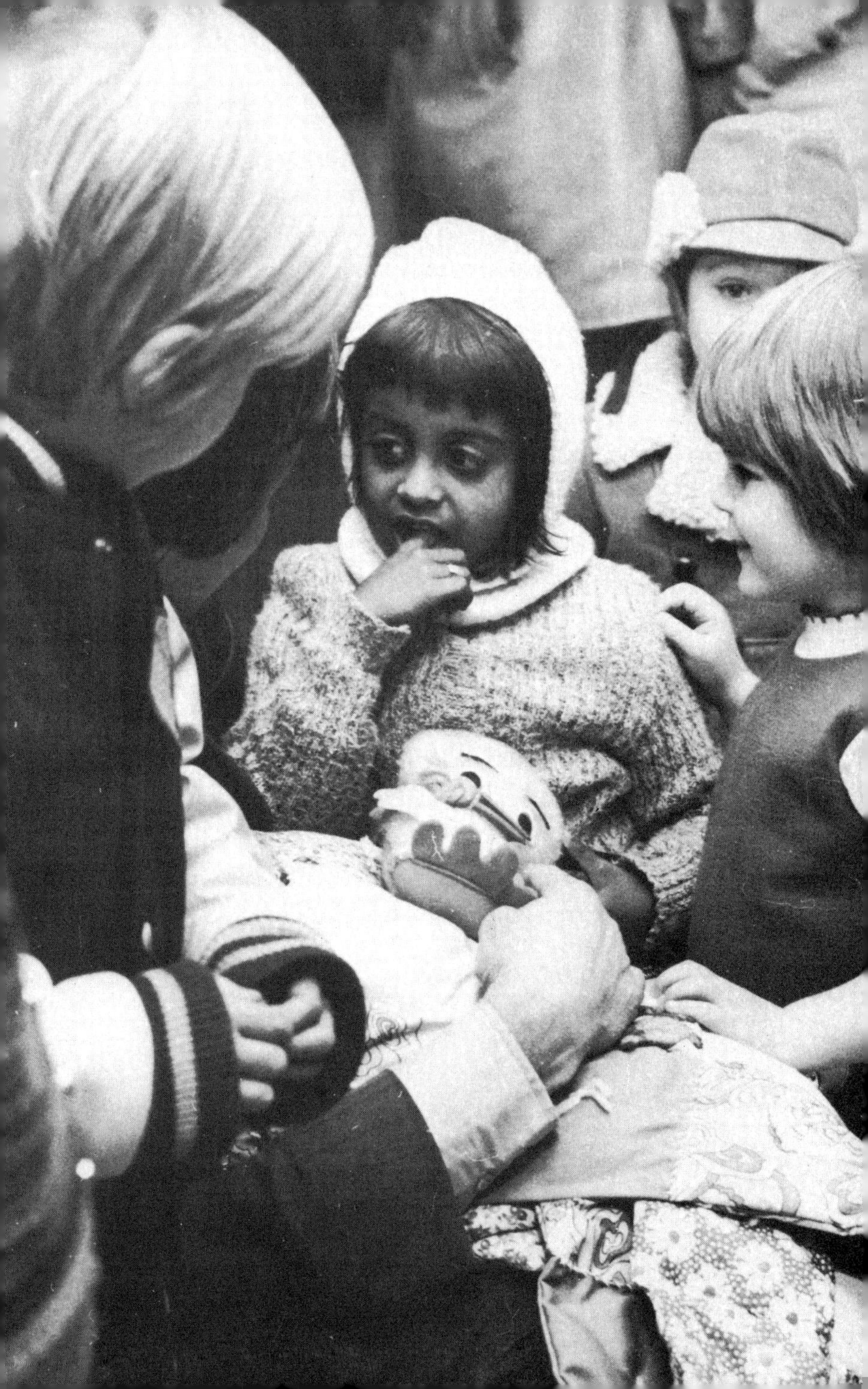

Adjusting to disappointment

I'm not extravagant
but I've had dreams,
plans for my future.
A golden flower would unfold
    possessions
    security
    travel.
I'm disappointed
because my future
won't be as I've hoped.
Rather, I will live with less.
My goal, my flower, is tarnished.

Disappointment is natural
but bitterness is vain.
Clinging to dreams
while ignoring present joys
or new horizons
could foolishly consume
my energy.
I shall design other goals,
set aside tarnished gold
which was more cosmetic than real.
My new flower can be
a fragrant, living,
beautiful creation of God,
rooted in trust more than security
and in living rather than gold.

Replacement values

When I feel like I'm giving up
the things that make me happy,
I need to remember
I can be happy in different ways
by choosing other things.
I pay the doctor less
because I choose to jog more
and eat better.
I find status
not from having a big car
but from having a small one.
I used to love a big hotel,
now I prefer camping.
I feel more joy on my bike
than in my car.
Once I liked "all new,"
now I enjoy "making do."
Replacing values
reduces the need to feel deprived.
I can replace consumption with conservation,
rehabilitation with prevention,
self-indulgence with sharing,
and self-centeredness with God.

Recycling is natural

The order of creation is remarkable.
Nothing disappears completely.
Fire and wood
turn to heat
    smoke
    carbon.
Leaves become humus for future growth.

The order of people
leaves much to be desired.
We do not honor the earth,
leaves to humus to trees.
We drop our litter
    our aluminum
    our glass and plastic
and hope it will disappear.

God watches our folly
and waits for us to realize
his world needs protection
and responsible care.
Recycling is consistent
with God's plan.
Am I part of the order of creation?

Conservation isn't easy

Our church is doing an energy audit.
It will cost a fortune
to insulate, improve;
to change this building
constructed in days of cheap fuel.
It's a beautiful building,
but wasteful.
What's especially hard
is the cost of change.
In times of greater expenses
it's hard to give more to the church.

Lord, you speak clearly to me.
Even a tithe is only a beginning.
If the church needs more
for wise energy conservation,
I must support that effort.
It is good stewardship of God's resources.
I can't rob people-program concerns
to pay for added energy costs.
I must go the extra mile
so that the church can continue to
    protect
    nurture
    love
    reach out
to the people of the world.
Give me the dedication I need.

Overcoming resentment

Some people don't have to
cut costs
or don't want to
conserve
and I resent their choices.
They disregard limits
and cause others to someday
have to limit themselves more.

Resentment is self-destructive.
I cannot change anything,
certainly not any person,
by harboring resentment.
Change myself.
Educate where I can.
Leave the rest to God.

We love to compete

From spelling bees to soccer,
we love to compete.
We cheer winners
and want to be near them.
We glorify the underdog
who comes from behind to win.

We are developing new games,
new ways to win
in a battle for survival.
We laud those who conserve most.
We join in the running game,
jogging
(without buying jogging shorts).
Everybody has a smaller car now—
    who gets the best mileage?
    who got their car first?
We compare electric bills
to see who has the smallest.
Our vocabulary goes from
biggest, fastest, and fanciest to
smallest, most efficient, and simplest.
We're still trying to win,
but the game is played
on different ground,
with different stakes.
One of the goals is cooperation.
It's ironic—
competing to see
who can cooperate best.

Doing things together

We do it together—
    a neighborhood picnic
    friends repairing cars
    our family going biking.
It's more fun.
We don't require that
every home have every tool—
we share!
We shovel walks together,
travel downtown together,
sings songs around the fire,
and go to church
together.
It is good for brothers and sisters
to dwell in unity
together.

I must tell the story

I'm quick to tell
tidbits of news
weather reports
discovered recipes.
I hold back statements
on opinions, issues.
But I have a story—
important
personal—
which I've kept to myself
too long.

Open up.
Tell the story—
excitement at success
challenge of tomorrow
relief of less stress
joy of deeper relationships.
What am I waiting for?
Other people want to know
how and why
changing my life-style
is good.

I'll change my plans

Urban planners
hardly hold a candle to me.
I try to plan everything—
cover all the bases
to avoid unexpected unpleasantness
    tardiness
    illness
    overdrafts
    death.
The world ignored my controlling ways
and life is changing around me
despite my plans.

Change plans.
Plan on lasting things.
Plan to love
regardless of irritability or income.
Plan to be grateful
for what there is,
whatever there may not be.
Plan to discipline myself
    to seek God
    to share my best
    to care.
Plan to believe and trust
because God's plan is supreme.

Finite

Funny word, *finite.*
It means having limits, boundaries.
What things are finite?
Oil and coal.
When I use gasoline,
it's gone.
It cannot be replaced.
Water,
spoiled by carelessness,
becomes useless.
Gone.
Coal to electricity.
Gone.
Finite.
Life, my life, is finite.
This existence on earth
ends.

What lasts?
Love.
Sharing,
because it can be
continued in the lives
of others in the future.
God is infinite.
Forever.
Always.
Hold on to what lasts
and share it—
God and love.